NATIONS IN CONFLICT

IRAN

by Sudipta Bardhan-Quallen

BLACKBIRCH PRESS

An imprint of Thomson Gale, a part of The Thomson Corporation

THOMSON

GALE

Detroit • New York • San Francisco • San Diego • New Haven, Conn. • Waterville, Maine • London • Munich

Photo credits:
Cover, © Reuters/CORBIS
© SEF/Art Resource,N.Y., 14
© Bettman/CORBIS, 11, 17, 18, 20, 23, 24, 27
© Jean Chung/CORBIS, 34
© Historical Picture Archive/CORBIS, 16
© Michael Nicholson/CORBIS, 15
© Reuters/CORBIS, 32
© Morteza Nikoubazi/Reuters/CORBIS, 36
© Christine Spengler/CORBIS, 25
© David Turnely/CORBIS, 6-7, 10
© Roger Wood/CORBIS, 8
© CORBIS/SYGMA, 21
© Mohsen Shandiz/SYGMA/CORBIS, 30
© Reuters/Landov, 41, 42
© Taherkenareh/Landov, 29
Lonely planet Images, 38
Stirnkorb Design, 5

LIBRARY OF CONGRESS CATALOGING-IN-PUBLICATION DATA

Bardhan-Quallen, Sudipta.
   Iran / by Sudipta Bardhan-Quallen.
      p. cm. — (Nations in conflict)
   Includes bibliographical references and index.
   ISBN 1-4103-0533-3 (hardcover : alk. paper)
   1. Iran—Politics and government—20th century 2. Iran—Politics and government—21st century 3. Islam and state—Iran—History. I. Title. II. Series.

   DS316.6.B365 2005
   955—dc22   2004029091

Printed in the United States of America
10 9 8 7 6 5 4 3 2 1

CONTENTS

The Two Faces of Iran

Iran is a country in turmoil. Change—and even revolution—has been a part of Iran's history for centuries. In fact, the name *Iran* was the result of a sweeping change in government that removed one monarch and established Iran's last dynasty. Throughout the country's history, different political groups have attempted to bring stability to the nation. Each time, the drastic changes brought with them their own challenges.

In 1997, Iranians once again voted overwhelmingly in favor of change—they rejected the guidance of their national religious leader, Ayatollah Ali Khamenei, and elected politicians who promised sweeping reforms to Iranian life, culture, and economics. Less than a decade later, in 2004, Iranians pulled their support from those reformist politicians and looked to new groups to bring about the changes they hoped for, such as strengthening the economy, putting an end to political strife, and restoring Iran's stature in the international community. Unfortunately for Iranians, it is still unclear how effective this new government will be in bringing about those changes.

As important as change has been, there have been constants in Iran's history as well. Most notably, since the seventh century, Islam has been an integral part of Iranian life, culture, and politics. It was the desire to give

religion a prominent role in government that led to Iran's Islamic Revolution in 1979. At that time, Iran became an Islamic republic, and the struggle for the people became balancing Islam's strict teachings and morals with life in the modern world. Clashes over how to achieve this balance have been a hallmark of Iranian life for decades.

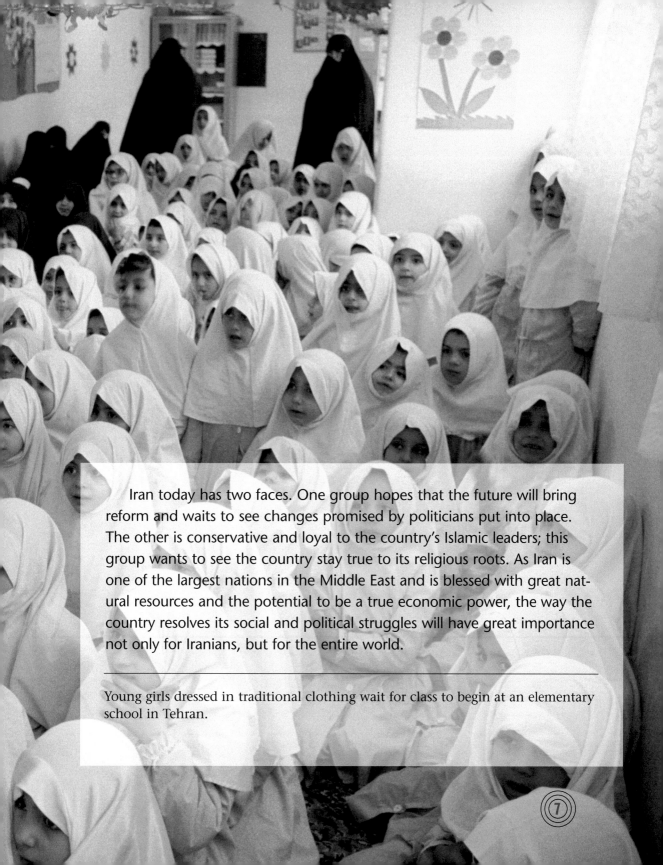

Iran today has two faces. One group hopes that the future will bring reform and waits to see changes promised by politicians put into place. The other is conservative and loyal to the country's Islamic leaders; this group wants to see the country stay true to its religious roots. As Iran is one of the largest nations in the Middle East and is blessed with great natural resources and the potential to be a true economic power, the way the country resolves its social and political struggles will have great importance not only for Iranians, but for the entire world.

Young girls dressed in traditional clothing wait for class to begin at an elementary school in Tehran.

CHAPTER ONE

Place, People, Past

The area of the world known as the Middle East is located in the southwestern part of Asia. With 636,000 square miles (1.6 million sq. km.) of land, about twice the size of Texas, Iran is the second largest nation in the Middle East. Iran is bordered by seven other nations—Armenia, Azerbaijan, and Turkmenistan to the north; Afghanistan and Pakistan to the east; and Iraq and Turkey to the west—and by the Caspian Sea, the Persian Gulf, and the Gulf of Oman. It is a land of diverse geography and diverse peoples.

Approximately two-thirds of Iran is desert regions and mountains. The climate is extremely variable—for example, during summer, temperatures can range from 35°F (2°C) in the northwestern mountains to 120°F (49°C) in the desert regions. Despite Iran's extreme terrain, the country's most valuable natural resources—oil and gas—flow freely from the land. Iran's main oil fields are found in the central and southwestern parts of the Zagros Mountains (in the northern part of the country) and in the offshore waters of the Persian Gulf. The petroleum industry is the economic mainstay of the nation, as revenue from oil accounts for 80 percent of all export revenue.

An oil refinery in northern Iran spews smoke into the morning sky. Oil is one of Iran's most important natural resources.

Although most Iranians are of Persian descent, the country's population includes a mix of many different ethnic groups.

The People of Iran

The people of Iran are as varied as the land itself. Today, more than 65 million people live in Iran. More than half of Iranians are of Persian descent, and they culturally and structurally dominate Iranian society. About a quarter of the population are Turkish-speaking Azeris. The rest of the population is a mixture of many different ethnic groups, including Kurds, Gilakis, Baluchis, Lors, Armenians, Mongols, Afghans, and Indians.

Much of Iran's diversity has come about because of its history. Although Iran is physically isolated from its neighbors by both water and mountain ranges, for thousands of years it was a crossroads between the Eastern and Western worlds. Ancient trade routes ran through the country, and the land was conquered by many different groups over the centuries. Iran's unique cultural variety is the result of this.

Despite the racial diversity, most people in Iran—over 95 percent of the population—share a common religion, Islam. This religious accord serves to unite the diverse peoples of the country. As Supreme Leader Ayatollah Ali Khamenei said in 2000, "The Turk and the non-Turk peoples of Iran are all brothers, Muslims and devoted to the Islamic system in Iran."[1]

Ancient History

The Islamic system and the importance of Islam in the daily life of Iranians is one of the defining characteristics of Iran today, but the religion itself is relatively new in the country. Iran, which was known as Persia before 1935, has a rich and vivid past. For centuries, the region did not practice Islam. In fact, Persia's history can be separated into two parts—the pre-Islamic period, during which the country was ruled by four different dynasties, and the Islamic period, which continues to this day.

During the pre-Islamic period, Persia was ruled by the Achaemenian Dynasty from 559 B.C. to 330 B.C., the Seleucid Dynasty from 330 B.C. to 170

Seleucus I was the first ruler of the Seleucid Dynasty, which controlled Iran from 330 B.C. to 170 B.C.

The ancient Persians practiced a religion known as Zoroastrianism. Here, a group of men takes part in a Zoroastrian ceremony.

B.C., the Parthian Dynasty from 170 B.C. to A.D. 226, and the Sassanian Dynasty from 226 to 642. All of these dynasties practiced an ancient Persian religion called Zoroastrianism, which was founded by the prophet Zoroaster in the 6th century B.C.

In 636, Arab armies ruled by the Umayyad Dynasty began to advance toward Persia from Syria. The Umayyads were an Islamic dynasty, set on establishing an Islamic empire. The last Sassanian monarch, Yazdegerd III, unsuccessfully attempted to fend off the Arabs. In 642, Persia came under Islamic rule.

Islamic Persia

Though the Persians believed that there would be religious and cultural tolerance under their new Islamic rulers, the Arabs began to systematically take apart the existing Persian culture. Arabic replaced the Persian language, Pahlavi. Persian buildings were destroyed and artwork was melted down to mint gold and silver coins. Islam replaced Zoroastrianism.

The Persians were, however, able to blend many parts of their old culture with the culture of the Umayyads. For example, mosques built after the Arabs conquered Persia shared architectural elements with Zoroastrian temples. When Islam replaced Zoroastrianism, the Persians altered the religion into something more familiar to them. According to author Richard Frye, Persia "accepted Islam but changed it by making of it an iranicized, international religion and culture not wedded to Arab . . . customs and beliefs."[2]

The Arab empire that was ruled by the Umayyad Dynasty was the largest state in history up to that point, and the Umayyads ruled Persia for a hundred years. However, in 750, the Umayyads were replaced by the Abbasid family as rulers of Persia. Further turmoil followed; over the next seven centuries, Persia was conquered again and again by different groups.

The Safavids and a New Persian Empire

Finally, in 1501, the Safavid Dynasty, which hailed from Azerbaijan, came into power. Their first shah, or king, Ismail I, overthrew Persia's rulers to found a new empire, which included all of present-day Azerbaijan, Iran, Iraq, and much of Afghanistan.

Safavid warriors battle the enemy in this seventeenth-century painting.

The Safavids were followers of Shia Islam, the minority branch of Islam. During their rule, Persia became the largest Shiite country in the Muslim world. Iran is still a Shiite Muslim country today.

Under the Safavids, Persia became a major imperial power, and the dynasty ruled for more than two hundred years. In 1722, however, the Safavid Dynasty collapsed. Their Afghan subjects successfully revolted against Safavid rule. Then the Afghans invaded other areas of the Safavid Dynasty and executed the last Safavid shah. As Frye writes, "Just as the Achaemenids ended with the foreign conquest of the [Seleucids], and the Sassanians with the Arabs, so the Safavid state fell to invading Afghans from the east."[3]

The Qajars

For the next five decades, Persia was in a constant state of turmoil. The country was finally stabilized under the Qajar Dynasty, which ruled from 1779 to 1925. The leader of the Qajars, Agha Muhammad, was able to reestablish the Persian monarchy.

Agha Muhammad did not rule for long. He was a cruel ruler, and his own servants assassinated him only a year into his rule. His nephew, Fath Ali, assumed the throne next, ruling from 1797 to 1834. During his reign,

Fath Ali partnered the monarchy and the religious Shia hierarchy. He gave Muslim clerics the authority to interpret religious law, to collect religious taxes, and to assemble small armies to enforce their religious judgments.

The support of the clergy helped strengthen Fath Ali's position as shah of Persia, but Persia was no longer in a position to be free of foreign influences. The years of political turmoil that preceded the Qajar Dynasty prevented Persia from modernizing and industrializing to the same extent that European powers had. Because European empires

Under the rule of Shah Fath Ali, Muslim clerics wielded tremendous power.

expanded throughout the world in the eighteenth and nineteenth centuries, Persia was left sandwiched between the growing Russian Empire in Central Asia and the expanding British Empire in India.

Foreign Influence and the Constitutional Revolution

In fact, Britain and Russia soon established strong presences in Persian trade and internal affairs. By 1890, the shah, Nasir ad-Din, was forced to turn to the British for military aid against the Russians, who repeatedly attempted to invade and conquer northern Persia. In return, Britain received special considerations in trade, such as the exclusive right to buy the entire Persian tobacco crop.

The Persian public grew increasingly upset with the foreign influence in their country's affairs. A revolt over the tobacco concession forced Nasir ad-Din to revoke it, but other revolts followed. A government proposal for increasing taxes, a general hostility to foreign intrusion in Persia, and corruption by the Qajar rulers led the public to demand great reforms.

A coalition of merchants, artisans, and religious leaders led the fight for constitutional reform. The Constitutional Revolution of 1906 established an elected assembly of legislators called the Majlis, limited the shah's powers, and made him subordinate to the Majlis.

In 1890 Shah Nasir ad-Din asked the British for military aid against the invading Russian army.

The Rise of the Pahlavis

The Constitutional Revolution did not bring stability to Persia, however. In 1908, Persia's shah, Muhammad Ali, attempted to override the constitution by disbanding the Majlis and arresting its members. He was deposed by constitutional forces and sent into exile in Russia. Though a new Qajar ruler was installed, from this point on the Qajars were nothing but figurehead leaders.

In the meantime, foreign influence in Persia continued to grow. During the Anglo-Russian Convention of 1907, Persia was divided into spheres of influence—the north for Russia and the southeast for Britain—without Persian consent. The two colonial powers had the final say on economic matters within the areas they controlled.

Colonel Reza Khan seized control of Persia's government in 1923.

Russian influence in Persia decreased in 1917 as the Russian Revolution raged. Eventually, Britain claimed all of Persia as a protectorate. It took greater control of Persia's economic affairs, including the lucrative oil fields. The Persian people were left without control of their own resources or goods.

Finally, British control over Persia was interrupted in 1921 when a Persian colonel named Reza Khan, with the support of the country's Muslim clergy, led a coup d'état and seized control of the government. Khan became prime minister of Persia in 1923, and by 1925 the Majlis had declared him the new shah of Persia. This began a new dynasty of rulers; Khan chose the name Reza Shah Pahlavi and began the Pahlavi era. In addition, just as he chose a new name for himself, in 1935 Reza Shah chose a new name for Persia—*Iran*.

CHAPTER TWO

Political Turmoil

When Reza Shah Pahlavi seized power in Persia, many Persians believed that he was strong enough to maintain order and bring stability to their country. At first, his autocratic rule was welcomed, as fear of his power guaranteed peace in Persia's streets. Reza Shah planned many reforms for Persia, mainly by breaking with Islamic traditions and modernizing Iran for the future.

Even though the Muslim clergy had helped Reza Shah gain control of Iran, he limited their powers and repealed laws based on the Islamic code of justice. This earned him the resentment of the clergy. In addition, Reza Shah required Iranians to wear Western clothes, and he withdrew government funding from mosques and Islamic colleges. According to author Robin Wright, "During his fifteen-year rule, Reza Shah was particularly contemptuous of religion: Islamic judges, taxes and laws were secularized, their replacements based on European models."[4]

As time went on, many of Reza Shah's decisions were met with resistance by the Iranian people. When the people protested, Reza Shah silenced them by using his military to suppress demonstrations and by

Reza Shah Pahlavi, shown here between two army officers, used military force to control the population.

Muhammad Reza Pahlavi became shah of Iran in 1941 after invading British and Soviet troops drove his father into exile.

imprisoning, exiling, or executing people who spoke out against him. As historian Roy Mottahedeh writes of a 1935 protest, "Angry crowds . . . came to hear preachers attack the policies of Reza Shah. When they did not disperse, Reza Shah's troops . . . opened fire. Over one hundred people were killed. . . . No further hostile religious demonstrations of any significance took place in Reza Shah's reign." [5]

Continued Foreign Intrusions

Reza Shah displeased his people, but he did not lose his throne until he displeased Britain and Russia (then the Soviet Union), the foreign powers who continued to influence Iranian affairs. Reza Shah wanted to share power with neither Iranian clerics nor foreign interests. He tried to limit foreign influence in the Iranian oil industry, but in 1941, British and Soviet troops invaded Iran and exiled Reza Shah.

Reza Shah's son, Muhammad Reza Pahlavi, was installed on the throne of Iran. Initially, it appeared that he was going to allow his people more freedom than his father had. Ultimately, however, Muhammad Reza Shah pushed for even more Westernization and modernization. In addition, foreign influence from a variety of Western nations peaked at this time from countries such as the United States, which lent the shah support in exchange for oil revenues.

Many Iranian people felt that their Islamic and Iranian identity was being threatened by the shah's attitudes and the influence of foreign powers. They felt that the shah was more concerned with appeasing other governments than looking after his own people. One of the shah's more outspoken critics was the Ayatollah Ruhollah Khomeini, a Shiite cleric and scholar. Khomeini said of Muhammad Reza Shah and his proposed modernization, "The son of Reza Shah has embarked on the destruction of Islam in Iran. I will oppose this as long as the blood circulates in my veins."[6]

Khomeini's Protests

Khomeini led a number of protests against the shah. Eventually, his opposition to Iran's government led to Khomeini's arrest and exile. Many Iranians, however, supported Khomeini and protested on his behalf against the shah. Even after Khomeini's exile, he kept in touch with fellow opposition leaders and kept informed about the political situation in Iran. When the shah did something Khomeini disagreed with,

As a young Muslim cleric, Ayatollah Ruhollah Khomeini protested the shah's plan for modernization in Iran.

AYATOLLAH KHOMEINI

Ruhollah Mousavi Khomenei was born on September 24, 1902, in Khomein, Iran. The study of Islam was a part of his life from the beginning, since his family had a long tradition of religious scholarship. His Islamic education began in a maktab, a traditional religious school, where Khomeini memorized the Koran. Later, he continued his education in Arak, where there were more opportunities for intelligent and promising young clerics. There, he studied with Ayatollah Abdolkarim Ha'eri.

When Ha'eri moved to Qom in 1923, Khomeini followed. He began as a junior figure in the religious establishment there, but became more prominent as time went on. For a long time, however, Khomeini was not a political activist. In fact, he took no stand against the Pahlavi government until 1962.

After the death of then leader Ayatollah Mohammed Boroujerdi, Khomeini emerged as an Islamic leader. He was soon accepted as marja-e-taqlid by many Iranians, and published many of his writings on Islam. Khomeini began publicly criticizing the shah. Eventually, his criticisms sparked the Islamic Revolution.

For a decade, Khomeini was the absolute ruler of Iran. As Middle East specialist Milton Viorst writes, "Khomeini consolidated his rule. Proving himself as ruthless as the Shah had been, he had thousands killed while stamping out a rebellion of the secular left. He stacked the state bureaucracies with faithful clerics and drenched the schools and the media with his personal doctrines. After purging the military and security services, he rebuilt them to ensure their loyalty to the clerical state."

On June 3, 1989, eleven days after an operation to stop internal bleeding, Khomeini died. He was mourned by millions of Iranians, and remains one of the most influential figures of the twentieth century.

For ten years, Ayatollah Khomeini ruled Iran as a dictator, executing anyone who opposed his government.

After fourteen years of exile, Ayatollah Khomeini returns to Iran in 1979 to take control of the government.

for example, when he established the Rastakhiz (Resurgence) political party in 1975 and required all adults to join, Khomeini responded from abroad. In this case, Khomeini forbade his followers to join the Rastakhiz Party by issuing a fatwa (an Islamic legal judgment).

Though Muhammad Reza Shah could not punish Khomeini in exile, he attempted to silence Khomeini's followers. Many of them were arrested and imprisoned. The more brutally the shah tried to suppress his opposition, however, the more Iranians resolved to support Khomeini.

Finally, in December 1978, as many as 17 million peaceful marchers protested against Muhammad Reza Shah. It became clear that the shah's position was precarious, and on January 16, 1979, he and his family fled Iran. Within two weeks, Ayatollah Khomeini returned from his fourteen-year exile and took control of the government.

Iran's Islamic Revolution

Later that year, the Iranian people voted for a constitution that made Iran an Islamic republic—a country governed by the mandates of Islamic religious law. They also chose Khomeini to be their Supreme Leader, or faqih and changed the official name of the country to the Islamic Republic of Iran. The Islamic Revolution had taken place.

The role of the faqih was central to Khomeini's new vision for Iran. He believed that "*faqih* should be not just one high official among the many who form the top echelon of the state administration but its supreme overseer, judge, and guardian."[7] Because of Khomeini's beliefs, the Iranian government was completely overhauled. The president no longer held any real power, having been replaced by the Supreme Leader. Khomeini established a new security force, the Revolutionary Guards, to help implement the changes brought about by the revolution.

Life in Iran was markedly different after the revolution. Westernization came to a grinding

Armed with automatic rifles, women in Khomeini's Revolutionary Guard patrol the streets of Tehran.

halt; in fact, much was done to reverse earlier Western influence, especially from the United States. According to Wright,

> Cultural outlets were forcibly closed. University life was suspended while curriculum was reviewed. . . . Religious vigilantes monitored morality in each neighborhood. . . . Even fashion changed. Women were forced behind chadors and hejab, the generic term for a variety of body covers. . . . To show loyalty, men grew beards. . . . Ties, the epitome of Western style, became taboo.[8]

Isolation and War

One of the most important results of Iran's Islamic Revolution was the country's isolation from the rest of the world, especially from Westernized nations. Khomeini wanted Western influences, which he felt were contaminating Iranian life, to be minimized under his regime, and he was successful. Iran's isolation was heightened after a November 4, 1979, incident in which Revolutionary Guards and Iranian students took hostages at the U.S. embassy in Tehran to protest the entry of Muhammad Reza Shah into the United States for medical treatment. In response to the hostage crisis, relations between the United States and Iran became hostile and mistrustful.

In addition, the internal turmoil in Iran continued even after Khomeini's revolution, partly because of an Iraqi invasion of the country in 1980. President Saddam Hussein of Iraq began the Iran-Iraq War in an attempt to lay claim to Iran's oil fields and to prevent the Islamic Revolution from extending into his country. Fighting continued for eight years, left more than 500,000 Iranians and Iraqis dead, and caused enormous damage to

In November 1979 demonstrators burn an American flag at the U.S. embassy in Tehran, where more than sixty American hostages were being held.

the infrastructures of both countries. Approximately 5 million Iranians were left without homes or jobs. Finally, a cease-fire was declared in 1988. Both sides returned to their prewar borders, and there was no clear winner.

After Khomeini

In 1989, not long after the end of the Iran-Iraq War, Khomeini died. Before his death, he supported a revision to the 1979 Iranian constitution. In 1979, the constitution had called for the religious leader of Iran (the marja-e-taqlid) and the political leader (the rahab) to be the same person. This was ideal for Khomeini, but it was unlikely that his successor could fill both roles

MOHAMMAD KHATAMI

Hojjatoleslam Seyed Moham-mad Khatami was born in 1943 in Ardakan, in the central Province of Yazd. His father, Ayatollah Ruhollah Khatami, was a respected cleric. Khatami followed in his father's footsteps by studying Islam. He attended the Qom Theology School, received degrees from Isfahan University and the University of Tehran, and finished his religious studies at the Qom Seminary.

Khatami became involved in political activities against Muhammad Reza Shah, and, for a time, he worked closely with Ayatollah Khomeini's son, Hojjatoleslam Ahmad Khomeini, to organize religious and political debates. After the Islamic Revolution, in 1979, Khatami became the head of the Hamburg Islamic Center in Germany.

In 1980, Khatami was elected to the Majlis as a representative from Ardakan and Meibod. By 1982, he had been appointed the minister of culture and Islamic guidance; he would serve in this same post again in 1989.

Khatami continued his political rise. In 1996, he became a member of High Council for Cultural Revolution by the Leader of Iran. Then, in 1997, he was elected the fifth president of the Islamic Republic of Iran.

Mohammad Khatami was elected the fifth president of the Islamic Republic of Iran in 1997.

Mohammad Khatami (right) is sworn in as Iran's president in 1997. He promised voters he would bring radical change to the government.

adequately. The 1989 revision separated these two roles. The Supreme Leader of Iran, the religious head of state, would now be selected by an elected body of Islamic scholars, the Assembly of Experts, from a pool of qualified clerics. The revision made the president, who was the political head of state, more clearly responsible for the daily operation of the government.

After Khomeini's death, conservative cleric Ayatollah Ali Khamenei was selected as the new Supreme Leader. At the same time, Ali Akbar Hashemi Rafsanjani was elected president. Many Iranians believed that Rafsanjani would be a bridge between the conservatives and the reformers in Iran. Rafsanjani wanted to increase employment, provide more housing, build new schools, and provide better medical services to the people of Iran.

Unfortunately for reformers, Rafsanjani faced a great deal of opposition from conservative members of the Majlis who refused to pass many of his reform proposals, claiming that they were too liberal. In Rafsanjani's second term as president, his relationship with Khamenei soured and he was even less able to enact reforms. Soon, life in Iran became more restricted—for example, even private activities such as watching programs on satellite television were declared illegal. For a time, it was unclear to Iranians or the rest of the world whether Iran was becoming a society with more freedom or whether it was reaching new heights in political and cultural repression. In addition, Iran's economy continued to struggle, and Iranians grew progressively poorer.

A New Leader for a New Iran

In 1997, Rafsanjani could not run for reelection because the Iranian constitution limited the number of terms a president could serve. A number of other candidates, including conservative cleric Ali Akbar Nateq-Nouri and moderate Mohammad Khatami, ran for office. Khamenei supported Nateq-Nouri, but even without the support of the religious establishment, Khatami won 20.7 million of the 29.7 million votes cast.

Khatami's triumph came as a surprise to many. People around the world believed that Iranians would vote as Khamenei bid them to do. However, the people of Iran, who hoped for reforms that would bring them more freedoms and a stronger economy, voted for the candidate that they believed would change their lives. As journalist Scott Macleod explains,

> Something was happening that Iran had never seen before. . . . Thousands of ecstatic Iranians overflowed into the dusty streets shouting, "Khatami! Khatami! You're the hope!" . . . Who voted for Khatami? Iranians fed up with political and social restrictions, women chafing at dress codes, twentysomethings denied satellite dishes and dispirited citizens who never saw a reason to vote—until Khatami came along.[9]

CHAPTER THREE

An Uncertain Future

From the beginning of his term, it was clear that Khatami faced many challenges in Iran. High unemployment, huge foreign debt, and high inflation plagued the country. Since 1979, the average Iranian's annual income had fallen from $1,200 to $800. Also, because Iran has one of the world's highest birthrates, approximately two-thirds of Iranians are under age 25, and without jobs or opportunities, the future is bleak for them.

Khatami tried to find a way to use his limited powers as president to bring about changes in his country. He was not very successful. The Supreme Leader and the conservative clerics, who still held the bulk of the power in Iran, often disagreed with Khatami's progressive views. In his first term in office, resistance from conservatives prevented Khatami from enacting many reforms.

Still, within the first eighteen months of Khatami's administration, he had done more than anyone since the Islamic Revolution to change Iran's image in the world. In 1998, at the opening session of the United Nations General Assembly, Khatami said, "If humanity at the threshold of a new millennium devotes all efforts to institutionalize dialogue, replacing hostility

Mohammad Khatami sought to change Iran's image in the world. Here, he addresses the United Nations in 2001.

Iranian voters line up to cast their ballots in the 2004 parliamentary election, when conservative candidates won the majority of seats.

and confrontation with discourse and understanding, it would leave an invaluable legacy for future generations."[10] Khatami even extended an olive branch to the United States, saying, "We need to create a pathway in the world of mistrust between the two countries. If we can remove the misunderstandings between people, we can remove the misunderstandings between nations."[11]

Khatami's Reelection

Despite resistance from the conservatives, the people of Iran largely supported Khatami. In 2001, Khatami was overwhelmingly reelected to the presidency, receiving 77 percent of the vote. Even reaffirmation of his popularity, however, did not strengthen Khatami's political position. For example, after the election, two seats on the Council of Guardians, a watchdog body that has the power to veto legislation, needed to be filled. Khamenei and the conservatives nominated two of their allies for the seats, but the reformist-dominated Majlis rejected the candidates. In response, Khamenei delayed Khatami's inauguration by three days until the dispute was settled. Khamenei ordered another vote, and the reformist lawmakers were forced to sit in angry silence as the two conservatives were confirmed.

This incident, and others like it, demonstrated a position that Khatami's allies maintained: that conservatives showed no sign of making concessions to the reformist movement, despite public support. As Morteza Haji, a close Khatami ally and current minister of cooperatives, explained in 2001, "[Khatami] faces increasingly serious challenges from those who cannot adapt themselves to reforms."[12]

Reforms at Risk

In fact, the challenges posed by the conservatives proved to be too great for Khatami to overcome. As BBC journalist Jim Muir writes,

> Reformist parliamentary bills were assiduously blocked by the Council of Guardians. . . . The hard-line judiciary kept the reformists on the political defensive through a series of arrests and newspaper closures. . . . The result was that the reformists had little to show for their four years in parliament and seven in the presidency, and the public largely turned away from them.[13]

Reformists protest the Council of Guardians, which disqualified 2,500 reformist candidates in the 2004 parliamentary election.

The March 2004 parliamentary elections resulted in an overwhelming win for Iranian conservatives. The era of democratic change that had been trumpeted by reformers seemed to be over—as Macleod wrote, "the power struggle in Iran—mullah warfare, some Iranians call it—is over, and the conservatives have won."[14]

One reason behind the conservatives' success is that they were able to manipulate Iran's laws to tilt the election in their favor. The Council of Guardians, for example, disqualified 2,500 candidates, most of whom were reformists. Included in the group of disqualified candidates were those who received the most votes in the 2000 election.

Another reason for the defeat of reformist candidates was that Khatami and his allies failed to change Iran in the ways that the people had hoped they would. Time after time, conservatives blocked reforms. Rather than mobilizing the Iranian people into political rallies and other shows of support, the reformists backed away from the confrontation. Immediately before the election, many reformist candidates who were not disqualified withdrew their bids for election to protest the actions of the Council of Guardians. They hoped this would rally Iranians against the Council of Guardians. The gesture, however, did not work. As Iranian political analyst Mahan Abedin explains,

> Those reformists who chose to boycott the election were still discredited by the fact that they had been unwilling to take such strong measures until the four-year-old conservative onslaught finally threatened their own re-election. By the time the noose finally closed around the reformers, the public had already grown indifferent to the plight of those who over-promised and under-delivered.[15]

The election results were devastating for Khatami and other reformists. As Muir writes, "With his supporters in parliament reduced . . . and only one year left in office, most analysts now regard President Khatami as a lame duck who may be able to exercise moral authority and keep the voice of reform alive in office, but will be unable to achieve anything more tangible."[16]

New Expectations

With their victory, the conservatives were faced with a challenge themselves—to fulfill the campaign promises that brought them into power. During the campaign, they pledged to improve economic conditions for all Iranians. They purposely avoided promoting religious principles in government. Many political analysts felt that these campaign strategies indicated that conservatives were willing to respond to public

Conservatives promised to improve Iran's economy and make goods like those for sale at this bazaar more widely available.

opinion. Since most Iranians have indicated that they want to move away from the repression that followed the Islamic Revolution and to move toward economic stability, many people feel that this will be the future course for Iran. According to Abedin,

> Some reformers predict that the new conservative deputies will have little option but to support policies adopted by the outgoing sixth Majlis to satisfy public demands. . . . The conservatives are unlikely to use their invigorated power to increase repression, which would unnecessarily alienate an already demoralized public. [17]

As for the reform movement in Iran, supporters contend that their efforts will not end with the 2004 election disappointment. Says Reza Yousefian, one of the reformist politicians who was barred from reelection, "If you interpret reform as a movement within the government, I think yes, this is the end. But if you regard it as a social phenomenon, then it is still very much alive."[18]

Building Bridges

Immediately after the election, many experts believed that the new government in Iran would try to further normalize relations between Iran and the United States and other Western nations. In order to follow through on one of the conservatives' core campaign promises, to create jobs for the thousands of young Iranians now pouring into the market, Iran would need foreign investment. Improving foreign relations with the West, however, will not be easy for Iran. There continue to be many hurdles in the way.

IRAN AND
THE WAR
ON TERROR

Another issue Iran faces on the international stage is how it will react to the U.S. war on terrorism. After the September 11, 2001, attacks on the United States, Iran made overtures to mend fences with the United States. It was the first government-to-government communication between the United States and Iran in twenty two years. Though Iranians by and large denounced the September 11 attacks, Iran says it will participate in an international coalition to fight terrorism only if the effort is led by the United Nations, not the United States. As NBC correspondent Jim Maceda explains, "Iran prides itself on leading Islam into the 21st century. Therefore, it cannot allow itself to be dragged into a war against Muslims—no matter how repulsive they might be—especially on the side of America, the former symbol of all things evil in post-revolutionary Iran."

On September 11, 2001, smoke billows from the north tower of the World Trade Center as a second hijacked plane strikes the south tower.

The U.S. government fears that nuclear energy plants like this one under construction in southern Iran are actually part of a program to build nuclear weapons.

For example, in 2002, it came to light that Iran had been secretly importing nuclear material and equipment for eighteen years. The United States and many independent experts believe that Iran is using its nuclear energy program as a cover for weapons development. Though Iran denies that it is trying to develop nuclear weapons, and though United Nations inspections have not uncovered conclusive evidence of an arms program, the threat of nuclear power adds tension to Iran's relationship with the West.

In November 2004, an agreement about Iran's nuclear program was reached between Iran, Britain, Germany, and France in which Iran would suspend its nuclear activities in return for improved trade and political relations. As U.S. State Department spokesman Richard Boucher commented, however, "Ultimately, it's what Iran does that matters, not just what they have agreed to."[19] It is still unclear how long Iran—which has long maintained that its nuclear program would be suspended only for short periods and only with the aim of building confidence between Iran and the international community—will accept all the limitations imposed by Western nations. More important, however, is that this is just one instance of many in which it is clear that the people of Iran remain conflicted about further cooperation with the United States and the West. Until this is resolved, the role of foreign nations in Iran's future remains uncertain.

The Fate of the People

While political powers battle over control of the government in Iran, average Iranians struggle to create better lives for themselves. The Iranian people have a history of rising up against repression and taking control of their country, but this history also includes the return of repression in other forms. Iranian politicians acknowledge this; in 2004, Muhammad-Reza Khatami, Mohammad Khatami's brother and the leader of Iran's biggest reform party, warned that Iran's future would be chaotic if conservatives in government continued to block the reforms Iranians demanded. He said, "if they [conservatives] stall reforms, then only two choices remain: dictatorship or uprising."[20] Perhaps the biggest challenge faced by Iranians today is how to find ways to keep from taking up arms once again and carry out their fight for reform peacefully, confined to the political arena.

Important Dates

559 B.C. – **330** B.C.	Persia is ruled by the Achaemenian Dynasty
330 B.C. – **170** B.C.	Persia is ruled by the Seleucid Dynasty
170 B.C. – A.D. **226**	Persia is ruled by the Parthian Dynasty
226 – 642	Persia is ruled by the Sassanian Dynasty
642	The Umayyad Dynasty brings Islamic rule to Persia
750	Persia is ruled by the Abbasid family; a period of turmoil begins as Persia is conquered again and again by different groups
1501	The Safavid Dynasty, headed by Ismail I, conquers Persia
1722	The Safavid Dynasty collapses; five decades of turmoil follow
1779	The Qajar Dynasty stabilizes Persia; Agha Muhammad becomes Persia's monarch
1797 – 1834	Qajar leader Fath Ali assumes the throne of Persia; Fath Ali partners the monarchy and the religious Shia hierarchy
1890	Nasir ad-Din grants Great Britain special considerations in Persian trade
1906	The Constitutional Revolution establishes the Majlis, limits the shah's powers, and makes him subordinate to the Majlis
1907	The Anglo-Russian Convention of 1907 divides Persia into spheres of influence without Persian consent
1908	Shah Muhammad Ali attempts to override the constitution but is deposed by constitutional forces and sent into Russian exile; Qajar rule becomes largely ceremonial
1921	Reza Khan leads a coup d'état and seizes control of the government
1923	Khan becomes prime minister of Persia
1925	The Majlis declares Khan the new shah of Persia, beginning the Pahlavi era
1935	Reza Shah Pahlavi chooses a new name for Persia—*Iran*
1941	British and Soviet troops invade Iran and exile Reza Shah; Reza Shah's son, Muhammad Reza Pahlavi, becomes shah of Iran
December 1978	Approximately 17 million peaceful marchers protest against Muhammad Reza Shah

January 16, 1979	Muhammad Reza Shah and his family flee Iran
February 1, 1979	Ayatollah Khomeini returns from his fourteen-year exile and takes control of the government
April 1, 1979	Iranians vote to make Iran an Islamic republic
November 4, 1979	Iranian students storm the U.S. embassy and take sixty-six people hostage
September 22, 1980	Iraq invades Iran and begins the Iran-Iraq War
June 3, 1989	Ayatollah Khomeini dies
July 1989	Ali Akbar Hashemi Rafsanjani is elected president
May 1997	Mohammad Khatami is elected president
June 2001	Khatami is reelected
March 2004	Conservatives win landslide victory in parliamentary election

About the Author

Sudipta Bardhan-Quallen holds a bachelor's degree and a master's degree, both in biology, from the California Institute of Technology. She is the author of several books, including nonfiction and picture books. She lives in New Jersey with her husband and two daughters.

For More Information

BOOKS

Cherese Cartlidge, *Iran*. San Diego, CA: Lucent Books, 2002.

Charles Clark, *Iran*. San Diego, CA: Greenhaven Press, 2002.

Miriam Greenblatt, *Iran*. New York: Childrens Press, 2003.

Masoud Kheirabadi, *Iran*. Philadelphia: Chelsea House, 2003.

Sandra Mackey, *The Iranians: Persia, Islam, and the Soul of a Nation*. New York: Dutton, 1996.

WEB SITES

The Iranian Cultural & Information Center (http://tehran.stanford.edu) This Web site was started at Stanford University in California to teach about the culture of Iran. It provides a wealth of information on Iranian culture.

The Iran Project (www.iranproject.org). A Web site dedicated to examining the changes in modern Iran.

Salam Iran (www.salamiran.org). Salam Iran is the Web site of the Embassy of the Islamic Republic of Iran in Ottawa, Canada, and provides a great deal of information on Iran.

Source Quotations

1. Quoted in Jon Hemming, "Iran's Azeris Want More Cultural Recognition," Reuters, June 3, 2001.
2. Richard N. Frye, *The Golden Age of Persia*. New York: Sterling, 2000, pp. 3–4.
3. Frye, *The Golden Age of Persia*, p. 4.
4. Robin Wright, *The Last Great Revolution: Turmoil and Transformation in Iran*. New York: Vintage Books, 2001, p. 45.
5. Roy Mottahedeh, *The Mantle of the Prophet: Religion and Politics in Iran*. Oxford, UK: Oneworld, 2000, p. 60.
6. Quoted in Baqer Moin, *Khomeini: Life of the Ayatollah*. New York: St. Martin's Press, 1999, p. 64.
7. Quoted in Mohsen M. Milani, *The Making of Iran's Islamic Revolution: From Monarchy to Islamic Republic*. Boulder, CO: Westview Press, 1994, p. 90.
8. Wright, *The Last Great Revolution*, pp. xiii–xiv.
9. Scott Macleod, "Iran's Big Shift," *Time*, June 2, 1997. www.time.com/ time/europe/timetrails/iran/ir970602.html.
10. Quoted in Wright, *The Last Great Revolution*, pp. 65–66.
11. Quoted in Wright, *The Last Great Revolution*, p. 68.
12. Quoted in Associated Press, "Iranian President Khatami Blasts Hard-Liners as He Is Sworn In," *Daily Texan*, August 9, 2001. http://tspweb02.tsp.utexas.edu/ webarchive/08-09-01/2001080903_s02_Iranian.html.
13. Jim Muir, "Analysis: What Now for Iran?" BBC, February 23, 2004. http:/news.bbc.co.uk/1/hi/world/middle_east/3514551.stm.
14. Scott Macleod, "Power of One," *Time*, March 1, 2004. www.time.com/ time/archive/preview/0,10987,1101040301-593571,00.html.
15. Mahan Abedin, "Iran After the Elections," *Middle East Intelligence Bulletin* 6, no. 2/3 (February/March 2004). www.meib.org/articles/0402_iran1.htm.
16. Muir, "Analysis: What Now for Iran?"
17. Abedin, "Iran After the Elections."
18. Quoted in Muir, "Analysis: What Now for Iran?"
19. Quoted in CNN, "Iran Agrees to Suspend Uranium Enrichment," November 14, 2004. www.cnn.com/2004/WORLD/meast/11/14/iran.nuclear.
20. Quoted in the *Economist*, "Iran in Turmoil," July 19, 2002. www.economist. com/agenda/displayStory.cfm?story_id=1246036.

Index